30 DAYS
TO OVERCOMING
ADDICTIVE
BEHAVIOR

TONY EVANS

HARVEST HOUSE PUBLISHERS
EUGENE, OREGON

Cover by Dugan Design Group

Heather Hair, Collaborative Writer

30 DAYS TO OVERCOMING ADDICTIVE BEHAVIOR

Copyright © 2017 Tony Evans
Published by Harvest House Publishers
Eugene, Oregon 97408
www.harvesthousepublishers.com

ISBN 978-0-7369-6463-0 (pbk.)
ISBN 978-0-7369-6464-7 (ebook)

Library of Congress Cataloging-in-Publication Data
Names: Evans, Tony, author.
Title: 30 days to overcoming addictive behavior / Tony Evans.
Other titles: Thirty days to overcoming addictive behavior
Description: Eugene, Oregon : Harvest House Publishers, 2017.
Identifiers: LCCN 2016030266 (print) | LCCN 2016037181 (ebook) | ISBN 9780736964630 (pbk.) | ISBN 9780736964647 (ebook)
Subjects: LCSH: Compulsive behavior—Religious aspects—Christianity. | Addicts—Religious life. | Habit breaking—Religious aspects—Christianity.
Classification: LCC BV4598.7 .E93 2017 (print) | LCC BV4598.7 (ebook) | DDC 248.8/629—dc23
LC record available at https://lccn.loc.gov/2016030266

Printed in the United States of America

20 21 22 23 24 25 / BP-CD / 10 9 8 7 6 5

CONTENTS

INTRODUCTION

Overcoming a stubborn addiction is not usually a process that can be accomplished in just 30 days. More often, it is a longer journey that we have to walk toward healing, and there may be a few stumbles along the way. But our greatest hope and power for the battle of overcoming our addictions comes from the One who walks beside us every step of the way. Jesus has promised that He will never leave us or forsake us. Instead, He offers this promise:

> Come to me, all you who are weary and burdened, and I will give you rest. Take my yoke upon you and learn from me, for I am gentle and humble in heart, and you will find rest for your souls. For my yoke is easy and my burden is light (Matthew 11:28-29 NIV).

Working through these 30 days will provide the tools you'll need to get on the right road and stay there. I cannot promise it will be easy, but I know you can get to a place of freedom. You might want to start reading this book again at the very beginning so that the powerful truths we have shared become more solidified in your heart and mind. And it is probably a good idea to find a wise companion for this journey of healing—a counselor, pastor, or mature friend. You don't have to do this alone!

It is my prayer that you experience God's strength and healing to help you overcome your addictions and find true freedom.

DAY ONE

A POW is a prisoner of war—a person who has been captured by the enemy and is held hostage in the context of a conflict. The opposing forces control the prisoner's living conditions, activities, and movements.

Many Christians live like POWs, but rather than prisoners of war, they're prisoners of addictive behavior. They have been captured by the enemy, and there appears to be no way of escape. They feel trapped in situations and circumstances that the world labels as addiction. Drugs, sex, pornography, alcohol, relationships, negative self-talk, work, food, gambling, spending…these things can become the go-to coping mechanisms for life's pain, disappointments, and boredom. When an action or activity begins to influence you more than you influence it, it can leave you feeling trapped—as if there were no way out.

I sometimes compare addictive behavior to quicksand. The harder you try to get out of a situation, the deeper you sink. Human methods and mechanisms can never set you free from a spiritual dependency. Rather, these attempts will make you sink faster, just as if you were struggling to escape from quicksand.

That's why I've chosen to focus on eight critical areas in which you must change your mindset in order to change your behavior. We often focus on behaviors instead of the root problems that cause the behaviors. But that does little good. As a man or woman thinks, so he or she is. In order to be set free from addictive behavior, you will need a change of mind. You'll need a new way of looking at yourself, God, others, and the things you do. Let's begin our month together with a word of prayer.

Heavenly Father, I lift up my friend in Christ to You today, and I pray that Your powerful Holy Spirit will use the words in this book to reveal and change any harmful thoughts coming from the enemy. As You have said, Your Word is powerful, like a two-edged sword. Please go deep into the beliefs and thoughts in order to dig up and remove any lies of the enemy. I ask that the blood of Jesus Christ and the power of His resurrection will be constant protectors during this time. May Your Spirit give the grace of discernment to separate Your truth from the lies that contribute to this addictive behavior. Thank You, Lord. In Jesus's name, amen.

DAY TWO

Satan's number one strategy to keep you in addictive behavior is to mess with your mind. He likes to plant thoughts in your mind, repeating them over and over until you start to think they are your own thoughts. When Satan told Eve she would be like God if she ate of the fruit, whose thought was that? Was that Eve's thought? No. That thought came straight from Satan himself. In fact, he'd had the same thought before, as we read in Isaiah 14:14: "I will make myself like the Most High." It was Satan's thought, but he planted it in Eve's mind.

If you've seen the movie *Inception*, you've seen this depicted dramatically. The movie is about planting a thought in someone's mind that will change the course of events for generations to come. It's a brilliant movie, and it helps us understand Satan's strategy for derailing each of us from our God-given destinies.

When you tell yourself, *I can't overcome this addiction*, whose thought is that? Or when you think, *I have to have this drink*, whose thought is that? Or when you entertain such thoughts as, *I am nothing. I have no value. I don't have power over my emotions. No one will ever love me…*who is doing the talking? We know these thoughts come from Satan because they are all lies, and he is the father of lies (John 8:44).

Satan has been working his deception for a very long time. He knows how to cleverly plant his thoughts in your mind and cause you to believe they are true. He did this to King David, as we read in 1 Chronicles 21:1: "Then Satan stood up against Israel and moved David to number Israel." Satan gave David the thought to start counting to see exactly how strong the nation really was. David decided to take a census, thinking this was his own idea. But taking this census was a sin because it demonstrated that David was relying on human strength rather than depending on God, and God judged Israel for David's sin.

We see another example of Satan planting thoughts in someone's mind in John 13:2. He "put into the heart of Judas" the idea to betray Jesus. In Acts 5:3, we see that Satan used the same approach with Ananias. Peter asks Ananias, "Why has Satan filled your heart to lie to the Holy Spirit?" In this case, Satan had given Ananias and his wife, Sapphira, the idea of selling a piece of property and giving some of the money to the church, pretending that they had given the full amount. This thought cost both of them much more than money. It cost them their lives.

How should we respond to Satan's thoughts? The same way Jesus did when Peter tried to keep Him from going to the cross. Peter told Jesus, "God forbid it, Lord! This shall never happen to You." To which Jesus replied, "Get behind Me, Satan!" (Matthew 16:22-23). The words came from Peter, but the thoughts came from Satan. When Satan gets your mind, he gets your actions. The key to overcoming addictive behavior is to take your mind captive.

DAY THREE

People who know me well know that I like to stay busy. I've always got something going on. But one thing you will rarely find me doing is being a handyman around the home. If something needs to be fixed, I usually call an expert to do it. I've learned the hard way that someone who knows what he's doing can do the job faster and even less expensively than if I went to the home-improvement store and tried to figure out how to do it myself.

Some home repairs can be complicated. Earlier this year, the electricity shorted out at our house and blew some fuses. Not only that, but when I called the electrician, he told me that the wiring in our home was so old that it was no longer safe. Our house is going on four decades old now, so things like this tend to break more frequently than they used to.

But can you imagine what would happen if I tried to restore our electricity myself? I'd probably electrocute myself in a matter of minutes. Not only that, I still wouldn't have solved the problem. Some issues are too complex and require too much expertise for me to fix them myself.

In Christianity, we have a lot of do-it-yourself believers. Too many people think that regardless of what may have led to the addiction, they can just pull themselves up by their bootstraps and fix the problem. In reality, addictions are almost always rooted deep within us at a level we may not even be able to identify on our own. That is why professional counseling is so important in helping us to identify and address the root causes of addictions.

Likewise, addictions are often so ingrained in our subconscious, mere willpower isn't enough to keep us from acting out when we become emotionally vulnerable. That's why accountability partners who are there to walk with those in recovery are such a critical part of overcoming addictions.

Not only that, but when you are seeking to overcome an addiction, you must keep in mind that apart from Jesus Christ, you can do nothing (John 15:5). You may have the correct spiritual lingo, but lingo only goes so far. Satan's primary tactic in the Garden of Eden was to sever Adam and Eve's dependence on God. He told Eve if she ate of the fruit, she could be like God (Genesis 3:5). Satan wanted humanity to operate independently of God, and that's what he also wants for you.

Your victory in overcoming addictive behavior must include a total surrender to God—to His way, His Word, and His sovereignty. It must include a total trust that He knows what is best for you and that He is in control—even of the things that have hurt you in the past. He has a purpose for your pain. And only He can lead you to it.

DAY FOUR

Satan wants to get ahold of your mind, but he doesn't plan on stopping there. His desire is to plant thoughts in your mind so they will take root and bear fruit in your actions. Scripture tells us that as a person *thinks*, so that person *is* (Proverbs 23:7). This passage is the foundation for overcoming all addictive behavior. Your addiction doesn't stem from the item or vice itself. It stems from your thoughts. Your addiction is rooted in your mind.

Once Satan plants thoughts in your mind, those thoughts then transfer biologically and physiologically to your emotions. Stick with me as we explore a little bit of science, because it's important for you to understand what is going on inside of you. Your *limbic system* is the system inside you that translates these thoughts into what are called *ligands*. Based on the specific thought, these ligands trigger a chain reaction of emotions similar to what you've experienced in the past.

Ligands are made up of *peptides*, *hormones*, and other bodily communicators. Once these ligands are released, they swim through your body toward their target receptors. This process happens almost instantaneously, which is why you can have a nearly automatic emotional response to a thought. Once the ligands reach their receptors, a vibration is made between the two of them, allowing the cells in that part of your body to open their walls and receive the message. This changes the cell itself, causing it to make new proteins, divide, or do any number of things, depending on the particular cells.

The process of thoughts triggering emotions can cause physiological changes, such as psychosomatic illnesses or even healings when given a placebo (a non-medicated substitute). It affects your mood and actions as your body responds to the emotion. Have you ever noticed how your entire body reacts when a car swerves toward you? Or when you sense something dangerous approaching you? And have you noticed how your body naturally relaxes when the danger is avoided? This is just a simple example of the way your body responds to emotions.

The devil wants to capture your thoughts because they trigger your emotions, which in turn influence your decisions. Addictions are prolonged by emotions. The alcoholism, drug abuse, endless shopping spree, excessive vacationing, or excessive work is a reaction to an emotion that has affected your body's cravings and needs. Understanding the physiological impact of your thoughts on your emotions and ultimately on your body helps to underscore where the battle for your freedom exists. It is entirely in your thoughts. Gain mastery of your thoughts, and you will master your emotions—and ultimately master any addiction you are enslaved to right now.

That's why you can't expect someone to make lasting changes just because you tell them to calm down or to stop drinking, cutting themselves, swearing, spending, or doing whatever they are doing. You can't talk someone out of an addiction simply by explaining the negative effects of what they are doing to themselves and those around them. You need to address their thoughts and get to the root of the lies that are causing the emotions that lead them to mask their pain through addiction.

The same holds true for you—you need to get to your thoughts and uncover the lies that must be uprooted and replaced with truth in order to stop your addictive behavior.

DAY FIVE

It's time to get personal. I'll share this with you because we often learn from the lessons of others, and I want you to get a greater glimpse into the impact our thoughts have on our bodies.

Anyone who knows me well would call me a workaholic. I love to work. If I'm not working, I'm usually reading books on the Bible, theology, and philosophy, underlining important points and recording my personal notes. I have thousands of notes (handwritten the old-fashioned way) inside my books and on notepads. If you walk into my office, you will probably see a stack of a hundred notes or so just sitting out—most likely because I've been looking at them while preparing a sermon or something I'm writing.

I love to work. And work is a good thing. It brings good to those who are impacted by it, and it gives me a deep sense of satisfaction. However, some time back, I began to notice a pattern creeping up with regard to my work and vacation schedule.

For about five years in a row, whenever I went on a vacation or took a break for Christmas and New Year's, I got physically sick. The sickness wouldn't always be the same thing, but the pattern of illness in general showed up almost like clockwork. Once I developed an abscess on a tooth. Other times I got the flu or had a persistent cough. Another time I developed gout and had to be in a wheelchair as we made our way back home through the airport. Yet another time I got kidney stones and had to be hospitalized. Whether severe or mild, something tended to creep up when I took time off from work.

On the other hand, I'm almost never sick while working. In fact, in nearly four decades of preaching on Sundays, I've only missed one Sunday due to sickness. This caused me to stop and think. Something was going on, and I needed to deal with it. In the process of examining my thoughts, I came to realize some important things about my view of work and rest. Some of those thoughts were good, and some were not. Eventually I was able to identify these thoughts and correct the ones that were not so good, and almost immediately I saw an improvement in my ability to rest.

I've been pretty much free of illness on vacations and holiday breaks for quite some time now because I addressed the root of the problem and not just the symptom. Overcoming addictions—to work, approval, drugs, alcohol, and so on—begins with identifying the root of the problem and addressing it in your mind. Addictions leave their impact in your life through broken relationships and broken bodies, so it's time to be set free from the symptoms of wrong thinking and get started on the path to wholeness and victory.

DAY SIX

I mentioned earlier that a counselor and an accountability partner can be great assets and can help you overcome addictive behavior. But I also want to point out that you cannot overcome your addiction by piggybacking on them entirely. They are there to help you process your thoughts in order to uncover the root issues as well as to keep you from acting impulsively when you are emotionally vulnerable. But the cure to overcoming your addictive behavior ultimately lies with you and God.

This is because only you control your thoughts. Only you have the power to continue shifting your thinking to a new place. When you rely too heavily on someone else during the process of overcoming an addiction, you can become addicted to that relationship. This is what we call codependency—your emotions and thoughts are now dependent on another person. In that regard, you are just trading one addiction for another. The final responsibility for victory in overcoming addictive behavior lies with you, not with your counselor or your friend.

When medieval fortresses were built, they were nearly impregnable. If you have toured overseas or seen them in movies, you know that their massive walls provided intimidating defenses against enemy soldiers on the outside. The task of scaling the wall in order to bring the fortress down was no small feat. Now, transfer this image of medieval fortresses to strongholds in your mind. These are the fortresses that Satan seeks to erect in your thinking in order to do his dirty work.

God says these strongholds have to be destroyed (2 Corinthians 10:3-5), which of course means He didn't build them. A stronghold is a negative, destructive pattern of thinking developed in our minds through repetition, traumatic experiences, or other circumstances. As the old adage says,

> Sow a thought, reap an action;
> sow an action, reap a habit;
> sow a habit, reap a character;
> sow a character, reap a destiny.

Once the stronghold is built, the enemy uses it to launch further attacks against your mind and repel your attempts to dislodge him. One reason strongholds are so powerful is that they are so entrenched.

Satan erects a stronghold when he convinces you that your situation is hopeless, that by nature you are a drug addict or an alcoholic or a negative person, that you are controlled by fear or shame, that nothing will ever change, and so on. Once you give in to and adopt this line of thinking, a stronghold is built, and your behavior will deteriorate because we always act according to who we believe we are.

You can tell when someone is under the influence of a stronghold. They may say, "I can't help myself," "It's not my fault," "I was born this way," or "I'm just a victim." When you view something as unchangeable that God says is changeable, the enemy has built a stronghold in your mind. It doesn't have to be anything as dramatic as drug addiction or alcoholism. Many of us have strongholds of anger, jealousy, or lust.

What can we do about these strongholds?

The only solution is to tear them down by "taking every thought captive to the obedience of Christ" (2 Corinthians 10:5). This is how to reprogram your mind.

DAY SEVEN

Do you know that it is possible to be delivered (saved) for eternity but be experientially undelivered on earth? It's true. This is because when you came to Christ for the forgiveness of your sins, God saved you completely (He justified you) for eternity. However, while you are still living on earth, He saves you progressively (He sanctifies you).

This is because our souls (the part of us that needs to be sanctified, or made right in our daily lives) are defective at our creation due to inherited sin. This is bad news—and it gets even worse. Our souls continue to grow and develop in unhealthy ways because of several factors, including our experiences, the information we take in, and our joys and pain. Every person's soul is distorted, similar to a television that is not able to get a clear reception. The image of God on our souls is fuzzy.

One of the major pitfalls people face when seeking to overcome addictive behavior is settling for what I call soul management—depending on behavior modification or their own willpower to make their souls better. This can include making commitments, attending seminars, listening to self-help gurus over and over again...even church attendance can become a soul-management tool. All these things can be helpful and add value to life, but they cannot ultimately fix your distorted soul. This is because your soul has been damaged due to sin, making the problem a spiritual issue rooted in sin. We know from Scripture that the wages of sin is death (Romans 6:23) and that sin itself produces death (James 1:15). In order to overcome sin's impact, your soul must be brought to the cross. You must, like Paul, choose to be "crucified with Christ" (Galatians 2:20).

We have all been damaged to some degree. In this, you are not alone. Psychologists tell us these days that more than three-quarters of all families would be considered dysfunctional. Yes, some of us have been damaged worse than others. You might be able to manage your soul better than your neighbor or coworker can manage his or hers. Maybe you have more self-control or personal discipline. But this might simply be because you have had less trauma or fewer negative experiences than they have. So it's really not fair to compare yourself to others. None of us are perfect—all of our souls are distorted to some degree.

But the solution to our souls remains the same. When you identify with Jesus Christ and His death on the cross, you do more than give a mental assent to the power of the cross. Rather, you abide in Christ's suffering, His mind, His words, and His thoughts on a matter. Without this abiding identity in Jesus Christ, you are bound by Satan's schemes. But when Christ's thoughts begin to dominate your soul, you will experience the new and abundant life He died for you to have.

John 15:7 says, "If you abide in Me, and My words abide in you, ask whatever you wish, and it will be done for you." This includes overcoming your addictive behavior. The key to your victory is in that verse—let Christ's words (thoughts) abide in you.

There are countless addictive behaviors, and one person's are usually different from another's, but similar strongholds are at the core of most of them. These include things like fear, insignificance, worry, doubt, personal identity, and low self-esteem. We may not mention your own addictive behavior in the following days' readings, but we will target the root beneath it as we see how to destroy common strongholds that trigger addictions.

In our remaining days together, I will give you the tools you need to be set free. But of course, I can't make you use them. My hope is that you will do more than read each day's statements of scriptural truth and personal truth. Rather, write them out and take them with you throughout the day.

Our brains respond to repetition, so by rehearsing and repeating these truths throughout the day, each day, you can plant them in your mind so they can take root. Eventually you will have replaced the weeds—the lies Satan has planted—with life-giving thoughts. We will spend a few days on each subject in order to cover it from different angles. These are the areas we are targeting: your identity, fear, worry, low self-esteem, hope, jealousy, contentment, and faith.

DAY EIGHT

Satan has a bag of tricks he uses to promote self-sufficiency and independence from God. One is probably his favorite because it's so effective. Satan wants to keep you spiritually off balance and defeated by creating confusion about your *identity*.

The devil wants sinners to think they're saints and saints to think they're sinners. If he can make you confused about your identity—if you don't know who you are—you won't know how to act.

How should we respond to Satan's deception? A good place to start is to become more aware of his strategies so we can be on guard against them. But more than that, I'm convinced we will never be truly free until we understand who we are in Christ and start living accordingly. We need to get our identity back.

The path to overcoming addictive behavior as a believer is the same route you took to become a Christian: complete dependence on Christ. Jesus did the work for your salvation on the cross. He will also do the work for your victory when you receive Him and His words, allowing Him to replace the lies and distortions in your soul with His truth and Spirit. As you read on in our time together each day, ask Him to show you your true identity as a believer, and then ask Him to empower you to live out that identity by the Holy Spirit's presence in your life.

Gracious Lord, thank You for rooting my identity
securely in the nature and perfection of Jesus Christ.
Thank You for forgiving my failures and sins through

His blood and righteousness. Let these words rest
deep within me, and may they go to work on my
behalf to unearth any lies, remove them, and replace
them with Your truth. In Christ's name, amen.

Scriptural Truth

If anyone is in Christ, he is a new creature; the old things passed away; behold, new things have come (2 Corinthians 5:17).

I have been crucified with Christ; and it is no longer I who live, but Christ lives in me; and the life which I now live in the flesh I live by faith in the Son of God, who loved me and gave Himself up for me (Galatians 2:20).

I am the vine, you are the branches; he who abides in Me and I in him, he bears much fruit, for apart from Me you can do nothing (John 15:5).

You have died and your life is hidden with Christ in God (Colossians 3:3).

You are all sons of God through faith in Christ Jesus (Galatians 3:26).

Personal Truth

- I am whole and complete because Christ is whole and complete.
- I am valued and loved in Christ.
- The Spirit of Christ in me gives me the ability to do anything He desires me to do.

- I can do all things through Christ in me.
- I am a child of God, a child of the one true King.
- I am not bound by old ways of thinking. I release them and replace them with the truth.
- My life is in Christ, and it is a good life.

DAY NINE

If you were to ask people, "Who is Angelina Jolie?" most would probably say she is a great actress and humanitarian. But is that really who she is? Acting and humanitarian work are not who Jolie *is*—they're just what she *does*.

Do you see my point? If Angelina Jolie's complete identity is wrapped up in her acting, what does that mean about anything else she does, believes, or values? And what if she were to retire? Would she cease to exist the day she retired from acting? Of course not.

That's why one of the greatest mistakes you can make is to define yourself by what you do. If your identity as a person is rooted in your performance, even if you're considered successful at what you do, you will be confused about who you are. This issue has an important spiritual impact because Satan knows that if he can keep you from knowing your true identity, he can hold you hostage to an ideal or image. He can prohibit you from living in light of your full spiritual victory, rights, and inheritance because you will be so focused on your accomplishments rather than who you are in Christ.

Your identity is always and only linked to your birth. Peter wrote, "Blessed be the God and Father of our Lord Jesus Christ, who according to His great mercy has caused us to be born again to a living hope through the resurrection of Jesus Christ from the dead." He later adds, "You have been born again not of seed which is perishable but imperishable, that is, through the living and enduring word of God" (1 Peter 1:3,23).

Your identity was determined when you were born into God's family and transferred into His kingdom. You are a representative of the King, an image bearer of the one true God. That's who you are. And every spiritual blessing you will ever need is tied to that identity.

Gracious Lord, remind me today in Your own unique way that my identity and self-worth are not tied to who I think I am, but rather to who I truly am in Christ. When my thoughts drift to doubt, I pray that You will give me a gentle nudge to be mindful that my value and significance come through my connection with Your perfect Son, Jesus Christ. Thank You. In His name, amen.

Scriptural Truth

Put on the new self, which in the likeness of God has been created in righteousness and holiness of the truth (Ephesians 4:24).

Blessed be the God and Father of our Lord Jesus Christ, who has blessed us with every spiritual blessing in the heavenly places in Christ (Ephesians 1:3).

God willed to make known what is the riches of the glory of this mystery among the Gentiles, which is Christ in you, the hope of glory (Colossians 1:27).

There is now no condemnation for those who are in Christ Jesus (Romans 8:1).

Just as the Father has loved Me, I have also loved you; abide in My love (John 15:9).

Personal Truth

- I am a child of the King.
- I am entitled to every spiritual blessing God has created for me in the heavenly places.
- My identity is fully formed and secure in Christ.

- Christ lives in me, the hope of glory.
- I am created to do good works and advance God's kingdom on earth.
- I have everything I need to fully live out my destiny.
- God loves me as His own, and I abide in His love.

DAY TEN

Galatians 2:20 is my life verse. It also contains a key principle for understanding your spiritual identity. This great verse says, "I have been crucified with Christ; and it is no longer I who live, but Christ lives in me; and the life which I now live in the flesh I live by faith in the Son of God, who loved me and gave Himself up for me."

According to Paul, you're dead. But the interesting part is, you are also alive through Jesus Christ, who lives within you.

Crucifixion means death. Whatever you were before you came to Jesus for salvation died with Him on the cross and was buried when He was buried. You are not a sinner saved by grace. You *were* a sinner saved by grace. Now you are a saint.

Believers are called saints 60 times in the New Testament. You might be an addicted saint, a defeated saint, or a sinning saint at some point in your life, but you are still a saint. You are "set apart" for God.

That name gives you great hope for changing your actions. Once you understand that you are a saint, you know to start from that mindset. You are not just a patched-up, converted sinner. You are holy in God's sight.

Think about the difference between caterpillars and butterflies. When was the last time you heard someone refer to a butterfly as a converted caterpillar? It *was* a caterpillar, but it has taken on a whole new character and a new name.

Before you met Christ, you were a spiritual caterpillar. However, when you put your faith in Jesus Christ, you became a butterfly. You are a saint. And as a saint, you have access to all power through Christ to appropriate His victory in your life and to live according to His plan for you.

*Gracious Lord, thank You for making me new in Christ
and giving me the chance to live a life of abundance
through the power of Jesus and His perfection. I turn my
thoughts from my mistakes and sins and place them on
Your Son, Jesus. Help me to die daily to my own self-doubts,
Lord, and to live daily in the purity and purpose that is
found in my Savior, Christ my Lord. In His name, amen.*

Scriptural Truth

In Him you have been made complete, and He is the head
over all rule and authority (Colossians 2:10).

By this the love of God was manifested in us, that God has
sent His only begotten Son into the world so that we
might live through Him (1 John 4:9).

All of you who were baptized into Christ have clothed yourselves with Christ (Galatians 3:27).

If you have been raised up with Christ, keep seeking the
things above, where Christ is, seated at the right hand of
God (Colossians 3:1).

We are His workmanship, created in Christ Jesus for good
works, which God prepared beforehand so that we
would walk in them (Ephesians 2:10).

Personal Truth

- I am a saint.
- I am baptized into Christ and clothed in Him.
- I am crucified with Christ, and I live through Him.
- I am a new creation.
- I am complete.
- I am whole.
- I am victorious.

DAY ELEVEN

Are you ready to learn how to tear down the stronghold of fear the enemy has built in your heart and mind? Jesus gave you the answer. You tear it down by changing your priorities. This is exactly what He was talking about in Matthew 6:33 when He said, "Seek first His kingdom and His righteousness, and all these things will be added to you."

In other words, if you will spend your time and energy aligning yourself with what God is doing in advancing His kingdom on earth, He promises to have your back with regard to the other things in life that might cause you to be afraid or worry. Jesus emphasized this when He said, "Do not worry about tomorrow; for tomorrow will care for itself. Each day has enough trouble of its own" (verse 34).

God gives you grace one day at a time. He will not give you tomorrow's grace today, and you don't need it. Why? Because His Word tells us, "His compassions never fail. They are new every morning; great is Your faithfulness" (Lamentations 3:22-23). So if you are fearful and concerned about what is going to happen tomorrow, you are essentially telling God that you do not trust Him. You are telling Him that He is not trustworthy. And you are sending your own thoughts into a cycle of pain and fear that will prolong your addictive behavior rather than helping you to overcome it. To be fearful about tomorrow is to lose your peace and victory today. Let it go.

Gracious Lord, help me to take notice when fear creeps up in my thoughts. Help me to catch these thoughts before they multiply and grow. Give me wisdom to discern what is rational and what is not, and in all things give me the ability to trust that You have my back. I want to turn my fears over to You, so please give me the grace to do that today and every day. In Christ's name, amen.

Scriptural Truth

God has not given us a spirit of timidity, but of power and love and discipline (2 Timothy 1:7).

[Cast] all your anxiety on Him, because He cares for you (1 Peter 5:7).

There is no fear in love; but perfect love casts out fear, because fear involves punishment, and the one who fears is not perfected in love (1 John 4:18).

Do not fear, for I am with you; do not anxiously look about you, for I am your God. I will strengthen you, surely I will help you, surely I will uphold you with My righteous right hand (Isaiah 41:10).

He who dwells in the shelter of the Most high will abide in the shadow of the Almighty (Psalm 91:1).

Personal Truth

- I am safe because God is watching over me.
- I am not alone.
- God strengthens me and helps me.

- I am loved by a perfect God, and perfect love removes all fear.

- God has given me a spirit of power.

- I am courageous.

- I dwell in the shelter of the Most High.

DAY TWELVE

What do you do when fear begins to consume your thoughts and won't let you go?

Scripture says that the best antidote to fear and anxiety is prayer. To see what is involved in prayer and what prayer can do for your fears, look at Philippians 4:6-7. Verse 6 says, "Be anxious for nothing, but in everything by prayer and supplication with thanksgiving let your requests be made known to God."

When fear grips you, begin by counteracting that fear with the truth of God. God says you must shift your focus because whoever or whatever controls your mind, controls you. God doesn't want you to be focused on your fearful thoughts and controlled by them. Rather, God wants you to focus on Him and to allow His Word and Spirit to control you. That's why prayer is so important. The formula here is simple. Be fearful about nothing, but pray about everything.

Philippians 4:6 uses the general word for prayer as well as the more specific word "supplication," which refers to asking for the answer to a specific need. Essentially that means you are to pray about everything, whether your request is general or specific. If you have a nagging fear but cannot seem to pinpoint what it is, take it to the Lord in prayer—He knows what it is. Or if you have a specific fear that you can see clearly in your mind, take that to Him too. Ask Him to help you remove your fears and replace them with His truth, and then thank Him in faith for doing that for you.

Gracious Lord, are not two sparrows sold for a cent? And yet You know everything that happens to them. You have also numbered the hairs on my head. Help me to take courage in knowing how well You know and love me.

Remind me today that I do not need to fear, because You are
ultimately in control of all things and You have promised
never to leave me or to forsake me. Thank You for Your
promises, which bring me peace. In Christ's name, amen.

Scriptural Truth

These things I have spoken to you, so that in Me you may
have peace. In the world you have tribulation, but take
courage; I have overcome the world (John 16:33).

You have not received a spirit of slavery leading to fear again,
but you have received a spirit of adoption as sons by
which we cry out, "Abba! Father!" (Romans 8:15).

Beloved, do not believe every spirit, but test the spirits to see
whether they are from God, because many false prophets
have gone out into the world (1 John 4:1).

Are not two sparrows sold for a cent? And yet not one of
them will fall to the ground apart from your Father. But
the very hairs of your head are all numbered. So do not
fear; you are more valuable than many sparrows (Matthew 10:29-31).

The Lord is my light and my salvation; whom shall I fear?
The Lord is the defense of my life; Whom shall I dread?
(Psalm 27:1).

Personal Truth

- I have peace in God.
- I have nothing to fear because the Lord is my defender.
- I am valuable to God.

- I am known.
- I am adopted by God and safe in His loving arms.
- I am fully cared for by a holy and powerful God.
- I have full access to God at any time in prayer, and I know He hears me.

DAY THIRTEEN

Have you ever ridden on an airplane through severe turbulence? The plane may have seemed to be out of control for a bit, and you probably got a little nervous. If your seat belt was already buckled, you may have tightened it. You probably held on to the armrest a little tighter. You may have felt a bit unsettled because you were momentarily suspended in the air. Perhaps you started reading the same line in your book over and over again because you were destabilized by the turbulence.

But then the captain probably made an announcement: "We've run into some turbulence, so we're going to adjust our altitude and try to find some smoother air." Now, your problem didn't disappear. The turbulence was still there. But you probably took a deep breath, relaxed, went back to reading, and generally felt much more at ease because you stopped focusing on the turbulence and focused instead on the pilot's announcement.

When you move your focus away from what you fear and redirect it onto God—the One who pilots our lives with surety—you will feel your fears subside.

Gracious Lord, when I am afraid, I want to put my trust in You. Will You please provide me with all that I need— the thoughts, truth, and encouragement—to actually do that? You are not a God of confusion, but rather a God of peace. When I am not feeling peace, I have distanced myself from Your presence. Empower me so that I will abide in You, Your words will abide in me, and I can fully experience Your peace. In Christ's name, amen.

Scriptural Truth

Though a host encamp against me, my heart will not fear; though war arise against me, in spite of this I shall be confident (Psalm 27:3).

When I am afraid, I will put my trust in You. In God, whose word I praise, in God I have put my trust; I shall not be afraid. What can mere man do to me? (Psalm 56:3-4).

God is not a God of confusion but of peace (1 Corinthians 14:33).

Immediately Jesus spoke to them, saying, "Take courage, it is I; do not be afraid" (Matthew 14:27).

Have I not commanded you? Be strong and courageous! Do not tremble or be dismayed, for the LORD your God is with you wherever you go (Joshua 1:9).

Personal Truth

- I am strong and courageous.
- I have courage.
- I am loved by a powerful God.
- God is not a God of confusion, but of peace.
- I have peace when I think of God's love for me.
- My fears do not control me.
- I trust in God, in whose Word I praise.

DAY FOURTEEN

Once there was a man who worried whether he would die of cancer because cancer was so prevalent in the society. He worried about it for 30 years—and then died of a heart attack as a result.

Should you be concerned about your health? Yes. Should you do the best you can to stay healthy? Absolutely. But after you've done all that you can do, don't worry. That's what God says. To worry is to insult Him.

To worry is to tell God you don't believe He is big enough, trustworthy enough, loving enough, or strong enough to see to the needs in your life. It is to question His sovereignty, His character, and His purpose.

Worrying is one of the most disrespectful things we can do to God because it calls His love into question. Keep in mind that He loved you enough to sacrifice His only Son on the cross in a humiliating and painful death in order to save you. That level of love should never be questioned through worry.

*Gracious Lord, You have told me to be anxious for nothing,
but in everything through prayer and supplication with
thanksgiving to make my requests known to You. When
I do this, You promise me peace. Lord, I ask that You
will intervene when my emotions get so strong that I
forget to do this. Remind me to do this and give me
the strength I need to obey You in times of emotional
vulnerability. Thank You. In Christ's name, amen.*

Scriptural Truth

Be anxious for nothing, but in everything by prayer and supplication with thanksgiving let your requests be made known to God. And the peace of God, which surpasses all comprehension, will guard your hearts and your minds in Christ Jesus (Philippians 4:6-7).

Do not be worried about your life, as to what you will eat or what you will drink; nor for your body, as to what you will put on. Is not life more than food, and the body more than clothing? (Matthew 6:25).

Peace I leave with you; My peace I give to you; not as the world gives do I give to you. Do not let your heart be troubled, nor let it be fearful (John 14:27).

Do not worry about tomorrow; for tomorrow will care for itself. Each day has enough trouble of its own (Matthew 6:34).

My God will supply all your needs according to His riches in glory in Christ Jesus (Philippians 4:19).

Personal Truth

- I am safe.
- I am provided for by a loving God.
- I am not alone.
- I am full of peace.
- I only need to focus on today.
- I am rightly related to God through Christ Jesus His Son.
- I am fully forgiven and loved.

DAY FIFTEEN

A man was in a hurry to catch an airplane. He ran through the airport, huffing and puffing, toward his gate. He passed a guy who was dressed in a pilot's uniform. The guy said to the breathless man, "Where are you in a hurry to?"

"I'm late for my plane," the man said. "I don't want to miss it." He proceeded to tell the guy what flight he was hurrying to.

The uniformed man said, "You don't need to hurry—I'm piloting that plane."

If the pilot is relaxed, you can relax too. Don't stress yourself out about things unnecessarily. Wait on God and trust that if He's taking His time, you can too. There is no need to worry over what you cannot control. Simply focus on today and the moment you are in right now—God has provided all you need for where you are right now. Trust Him and rest.

Gracious Lord, I want to trust You with all my heart instead of leaning on my own way of thinking. I know that if I do this, You will turn my worries into peace. I ask You to fill me with hope and joy, and help my unbelief. In Christ's name, amen.

Scriptural Truth

Be anxious for nothing, but in everything by prayer and supplication with thanksgiving let your requests be made known to God (Philippians 4:6).

What then shall we say to these things? If God is for us, who is against us? (Romans 8:31).

Seek first His kingdom and His righteousness, and all these
things will be added to you (Matthew 6:33).

Trust in the LORD with all your heart and do not lean on
your own understanding. In all your ways acknowledge
Him, and He will make your paths straight (Proverbs
3:5-6).

May the God of hope fill you with all joy and peace in
believing, so that you will abound in hope by the power
of the Holy Spirit (Romans 15:13).

Personal Truth

- I abound in hope by the power of the Holy Spirit.
- I trust in the Lord with all my heart.
- I acknowledge God in all my ways.
- If God is for me, who can be against me?
- God fills me with His joy and peace.
- God makes my paths straight as I look to Him.
- I have everything I need for this present moment.

DAY SIXTEEN

If you have young children, they probably depend on you to calm their fears after a nightmare or during a thunderstorm. They wake up, scream, and jump out of their bed. They run through the their bedroom, down the hall, and into your room. They jump in your bed because they need somebody to be with them.

Your hugging them doesn't stop the rain, thunder, and lightning, but it changes how they face it. They may fall asleep in your arms. Their fear, which filled them when they were alone, subsides when Mom or Dad holds them. You help them face their fears in the midst of their struggles.

This is exactly what your heavenly Father does for you when you face your own fears and worries. God may not stop the rain from pouring down on you, but He will provide the covering you need to keep you from getting drenched. Turn to God with your worries and allow Him to provide the security you need, both internally and externally.

Gracious Lord, assurance is a gift of Your Spirit that You give when I put my hope and faith in You. You said I only need faith the size of a mustard seed, so I ask right now for Your assurance that I can and will overcome this addiction by Your strength. Give me a deep sense of assurance and peace that it is done. In Christ's name, Amen.

Scriptural Truth

We know that God causes all things to work together for good to those who love God, to those who are called according to His purpose (Romans 8:28).

Faith is the assurance of things hoped for, the conviction of
things not seen (Hebrews 11:1).

Do not fret because of evildoers, be not envious toward
wrongdoers. For they will wither quickly like the grass
and fade like the green herb. Trust in the LORD and
do good; dwell in the land and cultivate faithfulness.
Delight yourself in the LORD; and He will give you the
desires of your heart. Commit your way to the LORD,
trust also in Him, and He will do it (Psalm 37:1-5).

The Lord answered and said to her, "Martha, Martha, you
are worried and bothered about so many things; but only
one thing is necessary, for Mary has chosen the good
part, which shall not be taken away from her" (Luke
10:41-42).

A bruised reed He will not break and a dimly burning wick
He will not extinguish; He will faithfully bring forth jus-
tice (Isaiah 42:3).

Personal Truth

- I am safe in the loving arms of God.
- I can trust God.
- I turn to God with my worries and fears.
- I know how to put my trust in God.
- I feel God's presence when I am worried, and He gives
  me peace.
- I am connected to the Source of peace and protection.
- I am well loved.

DAY SEVENTEEN

The story is told of a bear that lived in a cage that was 12 feet by 12 feet. It lived there for 12 years, so it got to know that cage extremely well.

The bear was so proficient at moving around its small world that it could close its eyes, walk to the end of the cage, and stop just before it hit the end of the cage. Then it would turn around and go to the other end. Before it hit the other end, it would spin around and do it over and over again, never ever bumping into the cage.

As it got larger, the bear's handlers decided to enlarge its world. They built the animal a new cage that was 36 feet by 36 feet to give it a lot more room. But when they put the bear into the new, larger cage, it continued to walk only 12 feet in one direction and then turn around to go the other way. The problem was, even though the bear had been moved to a new cage, it had brought the old cage with it. The bear was still controlled by the limitations of its old life.

This is how many believers are living the Christian life. They are living under the limitation of low self-esteem, but God tells us He loved us enough to die for us. That kind of love from the God of the universe is your answer to any esteem question you'll ever have. You are valuable. Live in the freedom and expanse of that truth.

Gracious Lord, thank You that I am fearfully and wonderfully made. Thank You for creating me with a purpose and a destiny. You love me with a love that is greater than any love I have ever known, and I want to live and walk in this truth. In Christ's name, amen.

Scriptural Truth

The LORD said to Samuel, "Do not look at his appearance
or at the height of his stature, because I have rejected
him; for God sees not as man sees, for man looks at the
outward appearance, but the LORD looks at the heart"
(1 Samuel 16:7).

You are altogether beautiful, my darling, and there is no
blemish in you (Song of Solomon 4:7).

I will give thanks to You, for I am fearfully and wonderfully
made; wonderful are Your works, and my soul knows it
very well (Psalm 139:14).

See how great a love the Father has bestowed on us, that we
would be called children of God; and such we are. For
this reason the world does not know us, because it did
not know Him (1 John 3:1).

The LORD your God is in your midst, a victorious warrior.
He will exult over you with joy, He will be quiet in His
love, He will rejoice over you with shouts of joy (Zepha-
niah 3:17).

Personal Truth

- I am of great value.
- I have tremendous worth.
- I am loved.
- I am quieted within by God's love.
- God rejoices over me.
- I am altogether enjoyed by God.
- I am the result of God's handiwork.

DAY EIGHTEEN

The great painter and sculptor Michelangelo came across a block of marble. He looked at the square block and said he saw an angel inside, waiting to get out. He began the chiseling process.

In the same way, God is at work in us. We are His workmanship.

You are His workmanship, and you are a masterpiece. Things may not be perfect in your life right now, but life is a process. God loves you so much that He is not giving up on you. He will continue to chisel and carve away what doesn't need to be there, and when He reveals who you truly are in Him, you will be amazed. Don't fight the process of personal and spiritual growth. You are worth the work.

Gracious Lord, before You even made me, You knew why You were creating me. You have a purpose and a plan for my life that will bring good to me, good to others, and glory to You. I want to live out that purpose, so I ask for You to empower me to overcome this addiction and anything else that is standing in my way of fully maximizing my potential in Christ. In Jesus's name, amen.

Scriptural Truth

Your eyes have seen my unformed substance; and in Your book were all written the days that were ordained for me, when as yet there was not one of them (Psalm 139:16).

You are a chosen race, a royal priesthood, a holy nation, a people for God's own possession, so that you may proclaim the excellencies of Him who has called you out of darkness into His marvelous light (1 Peter 2:9).

You were not redeemed with perishable things like silver
or gold from your futile way of life inherited from
your forefathers, but with precious blood, as of a lamb
unblemished and spotless, the blood of Christ (1 Peter
1:18-19).

God created man in His own image, in the image of God
He created him; male and female He created them (Genesis 1:27).

The Spirit of God has made me, and the breath of the
Almighty gives me life (Job 33:4).

Personal Truth

- I am made by the Spirit of God.
- I am a masterpiece.
- I am not dependent on any activity in order to cope.
- I am able to overcome any addiction.
- I am made in the perfect image of God.
- I am worth the work of refinement.
- I am chosen.

DAY NINETEEN

Yesterday we looked at an important truth from Ephesians 2:10, where we read, "We are His workmanship, created in Christ Jesus for good works, which God prepared beforehand so that we would walk in them."

The Greek word translated "workmanship" in this verse is *poiēma*, from where we also get our English word "poem." This word refers to a work of art, or a masterpiece. You are a work of God. You are His *poiēma*.

You weren't created on the assembly line or as a random object thrown together to fill up space or time. When God made you, He went to work, intentionally and delicately crafting your personality, looks, passions, skills—even your imperfections—into one magnificent work of art. He planted your dreams inside you and dreamed His own dream for you.

You are His masterpiece. You are God's dream. Therefore, you were made with a purpose. And that purpose includes authority. It includes dominion. It includes more than merely showcasing your talents. It involves impacting your world for good by ruling in the realm where God has positioned you.

> *Gracious Lord, my life is Your temple. My body and my mind house Your Spirit. I am made in Your very own image. You are complete and perfect, and You reside in me. You have blessed me with the honor of revealing You and Your love to those around me. Because of Your perfection, which lives in me, I'm stopping this addictive behavior, and I'm grateful that it no longer has power over me. In Christ's name, amen.*

Scriptural Truth

Just as a father has compassion on his children, so the LORD has compassion on those who fear Him (Psalm 103:13).

Since you are precious in My sight, since you are honored and I love you, I will give other men in your place and other peoples in exchange for your life (Isaiah 43:4).

Do you not know that you are a temple of God and that the Spirit of God dwells in you? (1 Corinthians 3:16).

We all, with unveiled face, beholding as in a mirror the glory of the Lord, are being transformed into the same image from glory to glory, just as from the Lord, the Spirit (2 Corinthians 3:18).

God, being rich in mercy, because of His great love with which He loved us, even when we were dead in our transgressions, made us alive together with Christ (Ephesians 2:4-5).

Personal Truth

- I have a great purpose.
- I am a work of God.
- God has a dream for me, and He wants me to fulfill it.
- I am being transformed into the likeness of God.
- I am capable of overcoming addictive behavior.
- I am greatly loved by God.
- I am precious in God's sight.

DAY TWENTY

Many of us have made them, and most of us will break them. They're our New Year's resolutions, and they can include being a better person, eating healthier, stopping this addictive behavior, memorizing Scripture, watching less football…the list is almost endless.

The simplest definition of a resolution is, "a firm decision to do something; a decree or promise."

Resolutions often resound with determination, bringing the hope of new beginnings. By May, most of them merely remind us that we didn't quite reach our goal. By December, the majority of us have forgotten what we had even resolved to do. But regardless of whether you have joined millions of others in making New Year's resolutions each year, I want to remind you that there is One who has kept every resolution He has ever made. He keeps His promises. He keeps His word.

And even if you are not able to stick it out in the gym, overcome this addictive behavior on your first try, or bite your tongue rather than beat others with it, He is able to do exceeding, abundantly above all you could ever imagine. And He has resolved that He has a great plan for you! Jeremiah 29:11 says, "'I know the plans that I have for you,' declares the LORD, 'plans for welfare and not for calamity to give you a future and a hope.'" Fix your eyes and your hope on the unchanging faithfulness of God, who has promised that goodness and mercy will follow you when you follow Him (Psalm 23:6).

I understand how easy it is to feel overwhelmed by something you just can't seem to beat. Things can feel hopeless. But if you will keep your eyes fixed on the Lord—and not on your addictive behavior—you will see that He who began a good work in you will also complete it.

Gracious Lord, hope comes from putting my trust in You. I am grateful for the hope You are giving me as I am overcoming this addictive behavior. Each new success provides me with new hope that I am that much closer to full victory. I can trust in the hope I put in You because Your Word tells me You are trustworthy. Thank You for letting me know I am no longer a victim to addiction, but an overcomer through Christ. In His name, amen.

―――――――――――――― Scriptural Truth ――――――――――――――

Many are saying of my soul, "There is no deliverance for him in God." Selah. But You, O Lord, are a shield about me, my glory, and the One who lifts my head. I was crying to the Lord with my voice, and He answered me from His holy mountain. Selah. I lay down and slept; I awoke, for the Lord sustains me (Psalm 3:2-5).

Let everyone who is godly pray to You in a time when You may be found; surely in a flood of great waters they will not reach him (Psalm 32:6).

Joshua then said to them, "Do not fear or be dismayed! Be strong and courageous, for thus the Lord will do to all your enemies with whom you fight" (Joshua 10:25).

When Jesus saw him lying there, and knew that he had already been a long time in that condition, He said to him, "Do you wish to get well?" (John 5:6).

The LORD favors those who fear Him, those who wait for His lovingkindness (Psalm 147:11).

Personal Truth

- I find favor from God when I fear Him.
- I am able to wait for God's lovingkindness to appear in my life.
- I am strong and courageous.
- I have a future filled with hope.
- I hope in God, who is worthy of my hope.
- I have a shield around my emotions; it is God Himself.
- I am sustained by God.

DAY TWENTY-ONE

God is so good at being God that He doesn't even need raw materials to work with. God can call into being "that which does not exist" (Romans 4:17). He can bring dead things to life. In fact, God is a master at bringing life to something that appears to have died. That is good news because if you have struggled with addictive behavior, it has likely impacted your relationships, your body, your work, and especially your hope. But God can create something out of nothing.

Never look at what you can see. Never look only at the facts. Trust in God. Do what Abraham did—hope when there is no hope around. In verse 18 of Romans 4 we read, "In *hope against hope* he believed, so that he might become a father of many nations." Doesn't that sound like a contradiction—hoping against hope? It was hope against all odds. That means Abraham hoped when there was no hope to be had. Abraham believed when he could see nothing to believe in. In a hopeless situation, Abraham hoped.

Paul wants us to clearly understand that it wasn't just a difficult situation that Abraham faced with Sarah. It was much worse than that. Abraham hoped against all hope. And because of that hope, Abraham took a step of faith—he took action based on that hope. Despite his age, he was intimate with his wife, and as a result, God gave them a child. Scripture says that when Abraham gave glory to God (verse 20) in the midst of his problem, he did what he needed to do. Nine months later, baby Isaac was born.

Abraham's response should be yours. Never let the problem dictate what you are going to do. Instead, act with a full view of the promise. And nine months later—or however short or long—you will be able to testify to what God has done in and through you.

*Gracious Lord, as I wait for You to move and work in
my life, You promise to give me new strength. Thank
You for this new strength, which enables me to take
one day at a time. I do not need to worry about
how I will face challenges in the future because my
victory is right now. Each moment of each day is
where I find You, and You are sufficient for each
moment of each day. In Christ's name, amen.*

Scriptural Truth

Hope deferred makes the heart sick, but desire fulfilled is a
tree of life (Proverbs 13:12).

[Be] rejoicing in hope, persevering in tribulation, devoted to
prayer (Romans 12:12).

May the God of hope fill you with all joy and peace in
believing, so that you will abound in hope by the power
of the Holy Spirit (Romans 15:13).

"For I know the plans that I have for you," declares the Lord,
"plans for welfare and not for calamity to give you a
future and a hope" (Jeremiah 29:11).

Those who wait for the Lord will gain new strength; they
will mount up with wings like eagles, they will run and
not get tired, they will walk and not become weary (Isaiah 40:31).

Personal Truth

- I gain new strength as I wait on God.
- I will not get tired when my strength comes from hoping in God.

- I have hope.
- I know my future is filled with good things.
- I am grateful for today.
- I know God has good plans for me to experience and live out.
- I am hopeful for a good day.

DAY TWENTY-TWO

Over the past 30 years, one of the highlights of my ministry has been serving as the chaplain for the NBA's Dallas Mavericks. If you have ever been to a professional basketball game, you know that each minute is filled to the brim with activity. Teams battle for the ultimate prize of being declared that night's victor. Players run, fake, block, and shoot in an effort to get one round ball through one round rim as many times as possible.

One of the elements of a basketball game that makes it so intriguing is the rebound. A rebound occurs anytime someone misses a shot or a free throw. In the case of an offensive rebound, someone on the offense grabs the ball after it bounces off the rim, and that player's team makes another attempt to score. Rather than allowing a change of possession, an offensive rebound maintains the team's control of the ball, giving them another chance to score.

If the game of basketball didn't have the option of the rebound, it would move a lot slower. The pressure underneath the basket would be nearly gone. And missed shots would be all the more painful. Essentially, an offensive rebound gives the shooter's team a chance to turn a bad situation into something good. It gives them an opportunity to get a hushed crowd back on its feet again.

What a rebound does in the game of basketball, God does in the game of life by giving us another chance after a failed attempt. A rebound in basketball is like a "do-over" in real life. It reminds us that it is never too late to try again.

It is not too late for you to overcome your addictive behavior and enjoy the full and abundant life Jesus came to give.

*Gracious Lord, all things are possible when I believe. That
includes no longer being bound by this addictive behavior.
For that I am thankful, and I give You praise for setting me
free from what used to dominate me. You are a strong tower,
and in You I find all that I need to cope with loss, pain,
and disappointment. Thank You, God, for being an ever-
present help in times of trouble. In Christ's name, amen.*

Scriptural Truth

And now, Lord, for what do I wait? My hope is in You
(Psalm 39:7).

And Jesus said to him, "'If You can?' All things are possible
to him who believes" (Mark 9:23).

Surely there is a future, and your hope will not be cut off
(Proverbs 23:18).

If we hope for what we do not see, with perseverance we wait
eagerly for it (Romans 8:25).

Blessed is the man who trusts in the LORD and whose trust is
the LORD (Jeremiah 17:7).

Personal Truth

- I hope with a heart full of gratitude and patience.
- I am blessed by God.
- I feel God's love throughout my day.
- I see God's hand moving things in my life for good.
- I choose to hope.
- I wait with patience.
- I know that God is trustworthy.

DAY TWENTY-THREE

Jealousy is a feeling of unease rooted in thoughts of rivalry, inadequacies, or the potential for loss. It can also be coupled with other emotions—resentment toward others, discontent with yourself, and so on.

The root of all jealousy is pride and selfishness. It is the opposite of the mindset God has called us to have—a spirit of humility and love for one another. That's why jealousy is such a dangerous sin. It can stall your growth as a believer and limit you from fully living out and maximizing your destiny.

How do you address jealousy? Galatians 5:26 tells us, "Let us not become boastful, challenging one another, envying one another." It is a reminder to us not to boast or challenge each other. We begin addressing jealousy by looking inside ourselves and making a true assessment of who we are. We are saints, but even on our best days, we might sin. Anything good that has come to you or me has been a gift of God's grace—and in that alone can we boast.

Gracious Lord, there is enough of You and what You supply to meet all my needs. Forgive me when I become jealous of someone else and what he or she has rather than being grateful for what You have given to me. Thank You for reminding me that You are my source and that if I need something—whether it's a material item or immaterial—I simply need to ask You in faith, believing that You will supply all my needs. In Christ's name, amen.

Scriptural Truth

If you have bitter jealousy and selfish ambition in your heart, do not be arrogant and so lie against the truth (James 3:14).

Where jealousy and selfish ambition exist, there is disorder and every evil thing (James 3:16).

A heart at peace gives life to the body, but envy rots the bones (Proverbs 14:30 NIV).

Wrath is fierce and anger is a flood, but who can stand before jealousy? (Proverbs 27:4).

You are still fleshly. For since there is jealousy and strife among you, are you not fleshly, and are you not walking like mere men? (1 Corinthians 3:3).

Personal Truth

- I know that all good things come from above.
- I am saved by a loving and gracious God.
- I have everything I need in Christ.
- I can celebrate other people's accomplishments.
- God has enough love for all of us.
- I strengthen myself by strengthening others.
- I am in the body of Christ as a member, not as the entire body itself.

DAY TWENTY-FOUR

One way to address the issue of jealousy in our lives is to look at what God has to say about pride, because pride is the root of jealousy. God hates pride. God loathes pride so much that Scripture tells us He even detests a proud look (Proverbs 6:16-17 NKJV). Pride was the first sin to disrupt God's creation, and it came from an angel named Lucifer.

Pride goes against everything God has done by taking credit for what only He could do. One thing God will never compromise is His glory. He will not share His glory with His created beings, which is exactly what pride wants. Humility is the foundation for all your power as a believer. In fact, Scripture tells us that before we pray, we are to humble ourselves (2 Chronicles 7:14). This is because humility recognizes our total dependence on God.

In seeking to overcome addictive behavior, let go of any notion that you can do this on your own. You are no match for the devil or his demons. But through Christ, you can do all things. Humble yourself—willingly come to Him and ask Him to take the reins of your heart, soul, mind, words, and actions. Release control to God through humility and watch Him do His work.

Gracious Lord, a heart of peace gives life to my body, but envy and jealousy produce cravings inside me that are worked out through addictive behaviors. I am grateful that You are replacing all envy and jealousy in me with satisfaction, contentment, and peace. I bless Your name, for You are my Source. In Christ's name, amen.

Scriptural Truth

Do not be overcome by evil, but overcome evil with good (Romans 12:21).

Hatred stirs up strife, but love covers all transgressions (Proverbs 10:12).

You shall not covet your neighbor's house; you shall not covet your neighbor's wife or his male servant or his female servant or his ox or his donkey or anything that belongs to your neighbor (Exodus 20:17).

Do not fret because of evildoers, be not envious toward wrongdoers. For they will wither quickly like the grass and fade like the green herb (Psalm 37:1-2).

I have seen that every labor and every skill which is done is the result of rivalry between a man and his neighbor. This too is vanity and striving after wind (Ecclesiastes 4:4).

Personal Truth

- I am content with my belongings.
- I have everything I need for today.
- I am grateful for the successes of my coworkers and friends.
- I am humble before God.
- I realize that all good things come from God.
- I understand my power is rooted in God alone.
- I am entirely dependent upon God.

DAY TWENTY-FIVE

Ultimately, jealousy is a reflection of a lack of contentment in our hearts and in our spirit. It is telling God, "What You have provided for me is not enough," which is a pretty harsh claim to make to a perfect God. Jealousy keeps us from taking responsibility for any lack we are experiencing in our lives and prevents us from addressing it. Instead, we blame the One who is never to blame.

God promises to meet all your needs. He promises to hear and answer the prayers you pray in faith. But He does not promise to have that faith for you. Only you can decide whether you will pray and live a life of faith and trust in God.

The next time you are tempted to feel jealous toward someone, pray instead. Ask God to show you—in a way that you will truly feel and know—that He loves you and that you are special to Him and also to others. Pray this prayer in faith, and He will do it. Life is not to be lived on a competitive plane. There is more than enough love, peace, and joy for all of us. So celebrate the successes of others as you look to God to affirm who you are in Him.

> *Gracious Lord, love is pure and peaceable. When I am jealous for the affection of someone or jealous of the attention someone else is getting, I am not living in love. Lord, I understand this leads only to lack and loss in my life instead of grace and peace, so in the name of Christ, I rebuke these emotions, and I draw to myself a heart of love, which comes from and also reflects You. In Jesus's name, amen.*

Scriptural Truth

Each one must examine his own work, and then he will have reason for boasting in regard to himself alone, and not in regard to another (Galatians 6:4).

[A servant] said to [the older son], "Your brother has come, and your father has killed the fattened calf because he has received him back safe and sound." But he became angry and was not willing to go in; and his father came out and began pleading with him. But he answered and said to his father, "Look! For so many years I have been serving you and I have never neglected a command of yours; and yet you have never given me a young goat, so that I might celebrate with my friends; but when this son of yours came, who has devoured your wealth with prostitutes, you killed the fattened calf for him" (Luke 15:27-30).

[Love] does not act unbecomingly; it does not seek its own, is not provoked, does not take into account a wrong suffered (1 Corinthians 13:5).

Make sure that your character is free from the love of money, being content with what you have; for He Himself has said, "I will never desert you, nor will I ever forsake you" (Hebrews 13:5).

Watch over your heart with all diligence, for from it flow the springs of life (Proverbs 4:23).

Personal Truth

- I am watching over my heart and my words.
- I am content with what I have.

- I know that God will never leave me or desert me.
- I celebrate the successes of others.
- I am happy for others when they are happy.
- I do not have to seek my own acknowledgment.
- I forgive others easily.

DAY TWENTY-SIX

Contentment comes naturally to us when life is moving along smoothly. But most people do not struggle with addictive behavior because life is moving along smoothly. Most addictive behaviors stem from a heart of pain, loss, or lack. Yet the Bible has a lot to say to us concerning how to be content even in the face of great loss and pain.

Job provides a great example of this contentment. Here was a man whose life had fallen apart. Amid the loss of his children and his property, "Job arose and tore his robe and shaved his head, and he fell to the ground and worshiped" (Job 1:20). He confessed that everything he had was from God, so God had the right to take it away. "Blessed be the name of the LORD," he concluded (verse 21).

Job knew where to turn when everything fell apart, and the Lord sustained him. But if Job hadn't experienced an inner connection with God and hadn't trusted in Him, he wouldn't have survived his ordeal. Even his wife advised him to curse God and be done with the whole mess (2:9).

When you choose to worship God during that time of greatest pain—and that might mean simply saying a prayer that acknowledges His control and sovereignty—you are taking your problem to God and replacing worry with contentment. This starts the process of replacing your negative thoughts (which would otherwise bring destruction to you) with positive, life-giving thoughts that produce life. Worship gives you contentment and peace in the time of trouble.

In a hurricane, heavy winds are all around. Yet there is always one peaceful spot, and that is in the eye. When Jesus Christ is the eye of your storm, you can have peace in the midst of trouble.

Gracious Lord, thank You for all that You have given to me. Thank You for waking me up this morning. Thank You for giving me a place to rest. Thank You for providing me with food to eat and air to breathe. Thank You for the ability to read and think. And thank You that in You I am no longer overcome by any addictive behavior. In Christ's name, amen.

Scriptural Truth

Not that I speak from want, for I have learned to be content in whatever circumstances I am. I know how to get along with humble means, and I also know how to live in prosperity; in any and every circumstance I have learned the secret of being filled and going hungry, both of having abundance and suffering need (Philippians 4:11-12).

Godliness actually is a means of great gain when accompanied by contentment. For we have brought nothing into the world, so we cannot take anything out of it either. If we have food and covering, with these we shall be content (1 Timothy 6:6-8).

Seek first His kingdom and His righteousness, and all these things will be added to you (Matthew 6:33).

Beware, and be on your guard against every form of greed; for not even when one has an abundance does his life consist of his possessions (Luke 12:15).

My God will supply all your needs according to His riches in glory in Christ Jesus (Philippians 4:19).

Personal Truth

- I am content with my life.
- I seek God first in all I do.
- My life consists of peace and contentment.
- I know God supplies all that I need.
- I have everything I need for this moment.
- I have access to God and His provision.
- I am grateful for God's provision.

DAY TWENTY-SEVEN

A lack of contentment is nothing new. In fact, Paul talked about it openly in Scripture. He called the art of being satisfied, or content, a "secret"—as if not many people know how to do it. We read, "I have learned to be content in whatever circumstances I am. I know how to get along with humble means, and I also know how to live in prosperity; in any and every circumstance I have learned the secret of being filled and going hungry, both of having abundance and suffering need" (Philippians 4:11-12).

For Paul, to be content is to have the resources available to you in order to handle whatever you are dealing with. In other words, you have enough for what you need at any given time, whether that enough is a lot or a little.

Contentment means being at rest and grateful for whatever situation you find yourself in. You can always know your contentment level by how much you are complaining and how much you are being grateful. If complaints are controlling you, there is no contentment. If gratitude is the dominant presence, contentment is there. Make an intentional effort today and this week to notice how many complaints fill your thoughts and words. That will show you how content you really are.

If you learn and apply Paul's secret, it will give you what you need to overcome any addictive behavior. Life has ebbs and flows. Sometimes you are up, and sometimes you are down. Sometimes things go your way, and other times they don't. Let Paul's secret of contentment be your dominant thought, expressing itself in gratitude, and your craving for your addictive behavior will diminish with time.

Gracious Lord, I ask for the grace of contentment in my life. I ask that You will bring me reminders of all I have to be grateful for. I ask that each morning when I wake up, Your Spirit will prompt me to thank You for something, anything. As I focus on what I'm grateful for, the longings for what I lack will diminish, and I will trust I am receiving all I need to overcome all addictive behaviors. In Christ's name, amen.

Scriptural Truth

As the Lord has assigned to each one, as God has called each, in this manner let him walk. And so I direct in all the churches (1 Corinthians 7:17).

The steadfast of mind You will keep in perfect peace, because he trusts in You (Isaiah 26:3).

I am well content with weaknesses, with insults, with distresses, with persecutions, with difficulties, for Christ's sake; for when I am weak, then I am strong (2 Corinthians 12:10).

Trust in the LORD and do good; dwell in the land and cultivate faithfulness. Delight yourself in the LORD; and He will give you the desires of your heart. Commit your way to the LORD, trust also in Him, and He will do it (Psalm 37:3-5).

Do not store up for yourselves treasures on earth, where moth and rust destroy, and where thieves break in and steal. But store up for yourselves treasures in heaven, where neither moth nor rust destroys, and where thieves do not break in or steal; for where your treasure is, there your heart will be also (Matthew 6:19-21).

Personal Truth

- I know God will give me the desires of my heart when I commit my ways to Him.

- I trust in God.

- My treasures are stored in heaven, and my reward is great.

- In my weakness, I find great strength in Christ.

- I am not alone.

- I delight myself in God.

- I commit my way to God.

DAY TWENTY-EIGHT

The Greek word translated "blessed," *makarios*, was once the name of an island off of Greece—Makarios Island. It was known as the blessed island because it was self-contained. The residents didn't need to leave the island in order to get their needs met. The island offered everything they needed. The natural resources of the blessed island were so thick, so rich, so fruitful, and so productive that everything they needed to enjoy their lives was already built in. The inhabitants of the island were self-sustained and self-contained without having to run to another island to get their needs met. The blessed island provided everything they needed.

Every addictive behavior that promises to satisfy you is outside of you. Whatever the substance or activity, it is outside of your spirit—your soul, which is the true essence of who you are. When you experience true blessing, you will be okay being on the island with God. Just being in the kingdom with the King puts you in a blessed location where you can feel content.

You know you *aren't* content (in the biblical sense of the word) when you have to keep leaving God and His provisions in your life to satisfy something in you. You need more than your relationship with God to have peace. You crave more than your communion with the Father to have satisfaction. Contented people find their sufficiency with Him. Look to God to satisfy you, and you will discover the key to overcoming addictive behaviors.

> *Gracious Lord, as I put my trust in You each day, I ask*
> *that You will give me favor and grow the level of my*
> *trust and contentment. I am strong in You, and in You*
> *I have all I need to overcome every addictive behavior.*
> *Thank You for this truth. In Christ's name, amen.*

Scriptural Truth

Give me neither poverty nor riches; feed me with the food that is my portion, that I not be full and deny You and say, "Who is the LORD?" Or that I not be in want and steal, and profane the name of my God (Proverbs 30:8-9).

An arrogant man stirs up strife, but he who trusts in the LORD will prosper (Proverbs 28:25).

The love of money is a root of all sorts of evil, and some by longing for it have wandered away from the faith and pierced themselves with many griefs. But flee from these things, you man of God, and pursue righteousness, godliness, faith, love, perseverance and gentleness (1 Timothy 6:10-11).

Better is a little with righteousness than great income with injustice (Proverbs 16:8).

You will make known to me the path of life; in Your presence is fullness of joy; in Your right hand there are pleasures forever (Psalm 16:11).

Personal Truth

- I am blessed with all spiritual blessings in the heavenly places.
- God makes known to me the path of life.
- I find fullness of joy in God's presence.
- I pursue faith, love, and gentleness.
- I am in charge of my own thoughts.
- I am choosing to trust in God.
- I am grateful for God's presence and provision.

DAY TWENTY-NINE

A man slid over the side of a cliff but was able to grab a branch at the last second. As he hung dangling over the precipice, hundreds of feet from the ground below, he screamed out, "Help me! Somebody help me!"

A voice came out of the sky. "Do you believe I can help you?"

The man responded, "Yes, I believe! Please help me!"

The voice came out of the sky again. "Do you believe I have the power to help you?"

"Yes, I believe! I believe! Please help me!"

"Do you believe I love you enough to help you?"

"Yes, I know You love me! Please, oh please, HELP ME!"

"Because you believe, I will help you. Now let go."

After a brief silence, the man shouted, "Is anybody else up there?"

Faith can feel just like that sometimes, can't it? Letting go of your addictive behavior can feel like letting go of the very thing that helps you to cope, gets you through each day, and sustains you. But God wants to know you have faith in Him, so He asks you to let go of the thing you seek the most as your source in life. He asks you to trust Him before you can see how He will deliver you.

Step out in faith and let go of your addictive behavior. It is not truly sustaining you. Rather, it's pulling you under. God will catch you when you let go and let Him be your Source. He is there. Faith will eventually lead to sight.

*Gracious Lord, through faith I have the power to
overcome addictive behavior. I choose today to no
longer doubt my own abilities but rather to place my
complete and total faith in You. Through You I can
do anything and everything. I am trusting in You
for the strength I need to make wise choices with my
time, thoughts, and body. In Christ's name, amen.*

Scriptural Truth

Truly I say to you, if you have faith the size of a mustard seed, you will say to this mountain, "Move from here to there," and it will move; and nothing will be impossible to you (Matthew 17:20).

Truly I say to you, if you have faith and do not doubt, you will not only do what was done to the fig tree, but even if you say to this mountain, "Be taken up and cast into the sea," it will happen (Matthew 21:21).

Immediately Jesus stretched out His hand and took hold of him, and said to him, "You of little faith, why did you doubt?" (Matthew 14:31).

Jesus said to her, "O woman, your faith is great; it shall be done for you as you wish." And her daughter was healed at once (Matthew 15:28).

They brought to Him a paralytic lying on a bed. Seeing their faith, Jesus said to the paralytic, "Take courage, son; your sins are forgiven" (Matthew 9:2).

Personal Truth

- I have great faith.
- My faith has the power to overcome anything.

- I am loved with an authentic love in Christ.
- I do not doubt the power of God in my life.
- My sins are forgiven.
- I am whole and complete in Christ.
- I am cherished by God Himself.

DAY THIRTY

One difference between God and us is that we have different viewpoints.

Consider a parade. We watch a parade progressively. We watch one band come after another. We watch the floats go by one at a time.

God sees the whole parade. He doesn't have to wait for each band to turn the corner. From start to finish, He sees the whole parade at once. He observes the whole package. That's why, "Without faith it is impossible to please Him" (Hebrews 11:6).

You've got to believe He sees what you can't. You've got to believe He's aware of everything—even things that aren't visible to you because you can't see around the corner. You've got to believe that He has a future for you, filled with purpose and with hope. That He will enable you to have the strength, determination, and grace you need to overcome this addictive behavior. And that you are worth a better life than what you may be experiencing right now.

Faith is the assurance of things hoped for. You may not see the "how" right now. You may not see the "why" yet. But if you will simply trust God in faith and approach today with that mind-set, He will get you through today. Don't look at tomorrow, for "tomorrow will care for itself" (Matthew 6:34). Just focus on living this day, this moment. That's all the faith you need—that God will get you through this moment. Take that faith with you as you enter the next moment, and so on.

In faith, you will overcome your addictive behavior with moment-by-moment victories that will add up to days, weeks, months, and years.

God is watching the whole parade. You can simply keep your eyes on what's right in front of you.

Gracious Lord, faith is the assurance of things hoped for and the conviction of things not seen. I am to walk by faith and not by sight. I choose to place my focus not on my external circumstances or my internal emotions, but rather on the power that comes through my abiding relationship with Jesus Christ my Lord. In Christ's name, amen.

Scriptural Truth

Faith is the assurance of things hoped for, the conviction of things not seen (Hebrews 11:1).

He has appeared in these last times for the sake of you who through Him are believers in God, who raised Him from the dead and gave Him glory, so that your faith and hope are in God (1 Peter 1:20-21).

...in the hope of eternal life, which God, who cannot lie, promised long ages ago (Titus 1:2).

We walk by faith, not by sight (2 Corinthians 5:7).

Whatever is born of God overcomes the world; and this is the victory that has overcome the world—our faith (1 John 5:4).

Personal Truth

- I can be sure of great things through faith in God.
- I am born of God and possess the power to overcome anything.
- I walk by faith and not by sight.

- I am dependent on my faith in every way.
- Faith makes me strong and resilient in times of trouble.
- I hope in God.
- I know God is trustworthy.

DR. TONY EVANS AND THE URBAN ALTERNATIVE

About Dr. Tony Evans

Dr. Tony Evans is founder and senior pastor of the 10,000-member Oak Cliff Bible Fellowship in Dallas, founder and president of The Urban Alternative, chaplain of the NBA's Dallas Mavericks, and author of many books, including *Destiny* and *Victory in Spiritual Warfare*. His radio broadcast, *The Alternative with Dr. Tony Evans*, can be heard on more than 1000 outlets and in more than 100 countries.

The Urban Alternative

The Urban Alternative (TUA) equips, empowers, and unites Christians to impact individuals, families, churches, and communities. TUA promotes a worldview that is thoroughly based on God's kingdom agenda. In teaching truth, we seek to transform lives.

The root of the problems we face in our personal lives, homes, churches, and societies is a spiritual one; therefore, the only way to address it is spiritually. We've tried political, social, economic, and religious agendas, but they have not brought lasting transformation. It's time for a kingdom agenda—the visible manifestation of the comprehensive rule of God over every area of life.

The unifying, central theme of the Bible is the glory of God through the advancement of His kingdom. This is the conjoining thread from Genesis to Revelation—from beginning to end. Without that theme, the Bible is a disconnected collection of stories that are inspiring but seem to be unrelated in purpose and direction. The Bible exists to share God's movement in history to establish and expand His kingdom, highlighting the connectivity throughout, which is the kingdom. This understanding increases the relevancy of these ancient writings to our day-to-day living because the kingdom is not only then; it is now.

The absence of the kingdom's influence in our own lives and in our families, churches, and communities has led to a catastrophic deterioration in our world.

- People live segmented, compartmentalized lives because they lack God's kingdom worldview.

- Families disintegrate because they exist for their own satisfaction rather than for the kingdom.

- Churches have limited impact because they fail to comprehend that the goal of the church is not to the church itself, but the kingdom.

- Communities have nowhere to turn to find real solutions for real people who have real problems because the church has become divided, ingrown, and powerless to transform the cultural landscape in any relevant way.

The kingdom agenda offers us a way to live with a solid hope by optimizing the solutions of heaven. When God and His rule are not the final and authoritative standard over all, order and hope are lost. But the reverse is true as well—as long as we have God, we have hope. If God is still in the picture, and as long as His agenda is still on the table, it's not over.

Even if relationships collapse, God will sustain you. Even if finances dwindle, God will keep you. Even if dreams die, God will revive you. As long as God and His rule guide your life, family, church, and community, there is always hope.

Our world needs the King's agenda. Our churches need the King's agenda. Our families need the King's agenda.

In many major cities, drivers can take a loop to get to the other side of the city without driving straight through downtown. This loop takes them close enough to the city to see its towering buildings and skyline, but not close enough to actually experience it.

This is precisely what our culture has done with God. We have put Him on the "loop" of our personal, family, church, and community lives. He's close enough to be at hand should we need Him in an emergency, but too far away to be the center of who we are.

Sadly, we often want God on the "loop" of our lives, but we don't always want the King of the Bible to come downtown into the very heart of our ways. Leaving God on the "loop" brings about dire consequences, as we have seen in our own lives and with others. But when we make God and His rule the centerpiece of all we think, do, and say, we experience Him in the way He longs for us to.

He wants us to be kingdom people with kingdom minds set on fulfilling His kingdom purposes. He wants us to pray as Jesus did—"Not my will, but Thy will be done." Because His is the kingdom, the power, and the glory.

There is only one God, and we are not Him. As King and Creator, God calls the shots. Only when we align ourselves underneath His comprehensive hand will we access His full power and authority in our lives, families, churches, and communities.

As we learn how to govern ourselves under God, we will transform the institutions of family, church, and society according to a biblically based, kingdom worldview. Under Him, we touch heaven and change earth.

To achieve our goal, we use a variety of strategies, approaches, and resources for reaching and equipping as many people as possible.

Broadcast Media

Millions of individuals experience *The Alternative with Dr. Tony Evans*, a daily broadcast playing on nearly 1000 radio outlets and in more than 100 countries. The broadcast can also be seen on several television networks, online at TonyEvans.org, and on the free Tony Evans app. More than four million message downloads occur each year.

Leadership Training

The *Tony Evans Training Center (TETC)* facilitates educational programming that embodies the ministry philosophy of Dr. Tony Evans as expressed through the kingdom agenda. The training courses focus on leadership development and discipleship in five tracks:

- Bible and theology
- personal growth
- family and relationships
- church health and leadership development
- society and community impact

The TETC program includes courses for both local and online students. Furthermore, TETC programming includes course work for nonstudent attendees. Pastors, Christian leaders, and Christian laity, both local and at a distance, can seek out the Kingdom Agenda Certificate for personal, spiritual, and professional development. Some courses qualify for continuing education credits and will transfer for college credit with our partner schools.

Kingdom Agenda Pastors (KAP) provides a viable network for like-minded pastors who embrace the kingdom agenda philosophy. Pastors have the opportunity to go deeper with Dr. Tony Evans as they are given greater biblical knowledge, practical applications, and resources to impact individuals, families, churches, and communities. KAP welcomes senior and associate pastors of all churches. KAP also offers an annual summit, held each year in Dallas, with intensive seminars, workshops, and resources.

Pastors' Wives Ministry, founded by Dr. Lois Evans, provides counsel, encouragement, and spiritual resources for pastors' wives as they serve with their husbands in the ministry. A primary focus of the ministry is the KAP Summit, which offers senior pastors' wives a safe place to reflect, renew, and relax along with training in personal development, spiritual growth, and care for their emotional and physical well-being.

Community Impact

National Church Adopt-A-School Initiative (NCAASI) empowers churches across the country to impact communities by using public schools as the primary vehicles for effecting positive social change in urban youth and families. Leaders of churches, school districts, faith-based organizations, and other nonprofit organizations are equipped with the knowledge and tools to forge partnerships and build strong social service delivery systems. This training is based on the comprehensive church-based community impact strategy conducted by Oak Cliff Bible Fellowship. It addresses such areas as economic development, education, housing, health revitalization, family renewal, and racial reconciliation. We assist churches in tailoring the model to meet specific needs of their communities while simultaneously addressing the spiritual and moral frame of reference. Training events are held annually in the Dallas area at Oak Cliff Bible Fellowship.

Athlete's Impact (AI) is as an outreach into and through sports. Coaches are sometimes the most influential adults in young people's lives—even more so than parents. With the rise of fatherlessness in our culture, more young people are looking to their coaches for guidance, character development, practical needs, and hope. Athletes (professional or amateur) also influence younger athletes and kids. Knowing this, we aim to equip and train coaches and athletes to live out and utilize their God-given roles for the benefit of the kingdom. We aim to do this through our iCoach App, weCoach Football Conference, and other resources, such as *The Playbook: A Life Strategy Guide for Athletes.*

Resource Development

We are fostering lifelong learning partnerships with the people we serve by providing a variety of published materials. Dr. Evans has published more than 100 unique titles (booklets, books, and Bible studies) based on more than 40 years of preaching. The goal is to strengthen individuals in their walk with God and service to others.

For more information and a complimentary copy of Dr. Evans's devotional newsletter,

call
(800) 800-3222

or write
TUA
PO Box 4000
Dallas TX 75208

or visit our website
www.TonyEvans.org

MORE GREAT HARVEST HOUSE BOOKS
BY DR. TONY EVANS

30 Days to Overcoming Emotional Strongholds

Dr. Evans identifies the most common and problematic emotional strongholds and demonstrates how you can break free from them—by aligning your thoughts with God's truth in the Bible.

30 Days to Victory Through Forgiveness

Has someone betrayed you? Are you suffering the consequences of your own poor choices? Or do you find yourself asking God, *Why did You let this happen?* Like a skilled physician, Dr. Tony Evans leads you through a step-by-step remedy that will bring healing to that festering wound and get you back on your journey to your personal destiny.

Watch Your Mouth

Your greatest enemy is actually in your mouth. Dr. Evans reveals life-changing, biblical insights into the power of the tongue and how your words can be used to bless others or to usher in death. Be challenged to use your mouth to speak life into the world around you. (Also available— *Watch Your Mouth Growth and Study Guide*, *Watch Your Mouth DVD*, and *Watch Your Mouth Interactive Workbook*.)

A Moment for Your Soul

In this uplifting devotional, Dr. Evans offers a daily reading for Monday through Friday and one for the weekend—all compact, powerful, and designed to reach your deepest need. Each entry includes a relevant Scripture reading for the day. (eBook only)

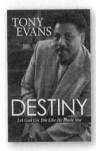

Destiny

Dr. Evans shows you the importance of finding your God-given purpose. He helps you discover and develop a custom-designed life that leads to the expansion of God's kingdom. Embracing your personal assignment from God will lead to your deepest satisfaction, God's greatest glory, and the greatest benefit to others.

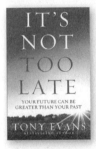

It's Not Too Late

Dr. Evans uses prominent Bible characters to show that God delights in using imperfect people who have failed, sinned, or just plain blown it. You'll be encouraged as you come to understand that God has you, too, on a path to success *despite* your imperfections and mistakes.

The Power of God's Names

Dr. Evans shows that it's through the names of God that the nature of God is revealed. By understanding the characteristics of God as revealed through His names, you will be better equipped to face the challenges life throws at you.

Praying Through the Names of God

Dr. Evans reveals insights into some of God's powerful names and provides prayers based on those names. Your prayer life will be revitalized as you connect your needs with the relevant characteristics of His names.

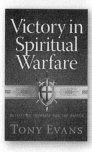

Victory in Spiritual Warfare

Dr. Evans demystifies spiritual warfare and empowers you with a life-changing truth: Every struggle faced in the physical realm has its root in the spiritual realm. With passion and practicality, Dr. Evans shows you how to live a transformed life in and through the power of Christ's victory.

Prayers for Victory in Spiritual Warfare

Feel defeated? God has given you powerful weapons to help you withstand the onslaught of Satan's lies. This book of prayers, based on Dr. Evans's life-changing book *Victory in Spiritual Warfare*, will help you stand against the enemy's attacks.

Horizontal Jesus

Do you want to sense God's encouragement, comfort, and love for you every day? Dr. Tony Evans reveals that as you live like a horizontal Jesus—giving these things away to others—you will personally experience them with God like never before. (Also available—*Horizontal Jesus Study Guide*.)

To learn more about Harvest House books and
to read sample chapters, visit our website:

www.harvesthousepublishers.com

HARVEST HOUSE PUBLISHERS
EUGENE, OREGON